The CUSTOMER SERVICE COMPANION

The Essential Handbook For Those Who Serve Others

C. Leslie Charles

Yes! Press
East Lansing, Michigan

Printed in the United States of America

Published by:

Yes! Press
PO Box 956
East Lansing, MI 48826
517-675-7535

Cover Design by Diana L.Grinwis
Cover Portrait by Kim Kauffman
Graphics by Kathryn Darnell

Publisher's Cataloging in Publication Data

Charles, C. Leslie.
    The customer service companion : the essential handbook for
those who serve others / C. Leslie Charles.
    p. cm
    ISBN 0-9644621-1-7

    1. Customer services--Handbooks, manuals, etc. 2. Customer
relations--Handbooks, manuals, etc. I. Title

HF5415.5.C43 1996   658.8'12
                                 QB196-40298

Library of Congress Catalog Card Number 96-90171

First Edition
10 9 8 7 6 5 4 3

Dedication

With appreciation to my clients who strive for
service excellence, and every individual who
has given me the gift of superlative service in
businesses, schools, restaurants, hotels,
hospitals, veterinary, medical or dental offices,
financial institutions, associations, and
government agencies; far too many to name
(you know who you are). And to those who
have given me lousy service, thanks for
providing the inspiration to write this book.

Contents

∞

The Essentials of Service

Quick Reminders on Customer Service
Pages 104 ~ 149

Service Skills in Action

*The Essential Handbook
For Those Who Serve Others*

Directions:

Open book
Apply liberally to brain
Read and repeat

Introduction

As a customer, it's often not the product but the service that drives you crazy. Just yesterday we called in our lunch order to a local sandwich shop and our office manager, Lois, went to pick up our sandwiches at the appointed time.

After waiting in line and hearing someone shout, "Lisa, your order's ready!" for the third time, she asked, "Could that order possibly be for Lois?" "Oh. Yeah." came the reply.

She returned to the office muttering, "Let's not go there any more, they always get something mixed up!" Their food is good, their selection is interesting, and they're on the verge of losing a customer.

You've seen many books about providing exceptional customer service, maybe you've even read a few. None are like the one you're reading now. It is different in three ways.

First, it's practical. You won't have to wade

through theory to get ideas that will work in your world. From the first page you'll gather suggestions you can put to use at once.

Second, you'll actually read it. Open up to any page and you'll immediately be struck by the author's warm and welcoming voice. Don't limit yourself to reading this book from the front to the back. This is a book meant to be dabbled in.

Pick a page at random. Underline the sentence that speaks to you. Dog-ear the pages that you want to read again. Keep your copy on your desk and you'll find yourself using it again and again. It's the perfect start for a new day; your resource to help clarify difficult encounters, and to offer the words of encouragement you need when the going gets tough.

Third, it's written by C. Leslie Charles. Leslie can walk into any business and lift the spirits and sharpen the skills of those dealing directly with the customer; I've seen her do it.

She understands the reality of front line

customer service jobs—from the excitement of solving a customer's problem to the frustration one feels when the organization seems not to care. As she was writing *The Customer Service Companion*, Leslie was thinking of you and the thousands of Customer Service Professionals she's encouraged, trained, and counseled over the past twenty years.

Remember our local sandwich shop? We've decided to give them one more try. Only this time, when Lois picks up the order she'll be leaving them a copy of this book. They need to read *The Customer Service Companion*.

September 1996
Chris Clarke-Epstein, CSP
Author of *Simple Encounters*

Author's Notes: How to use this book

Whether you bought this book for yourself or it was provided for you, think of it as a personal gift. As its name implies, it is *your* companion. Keep it on your desk; carry it with you. Browse through it on your break or when you feel as if you "just can't take it any more." Use it for ideas on how to handle common frustrations with an uncommonly positive attitude.

Read it when you need a quick refresher course or a reminder of what's right in the world. Use it to set your mood as you begin a work day, or as a personal haven in the middle of a hectic one. Put tabs on the pages you think you'll use most.

The Customer Service Companion is a complete seminar in book form, designed to be enjoyable, easy to read, and effective. Use it as a mental tool. Write in it—jot down your favorite ideas, make personal notes, or record some of your own service experiences.

This is your book, your companion; a guide, a manual, a handbook, and, if you wish, a journal. Here's to you—and to better service for us all!

The
Essentials of Service

*Serving others well
serves you well.
The effort you expend
helping others pays off
more for you
than anyone else.*

—C. Leslie Charles

1.

Customer Service:
You Know "The Secret"

We are all customers, and we all have customers. In fact, your experiences as a customer, the lessons you've learned, both good and bad, have made you an expert on service. You know the secret to giving good service, and you learned it long ago.

As a consumer, you've been served well and served poorly. You know how you want to be treated and how you don't. You know, firsthand, how an employee's positive or negative attitude can affect you. This awareness can help you in your work every day.

When it comes to service, most of us know what we should do, but doing it consistently is tough. Yet, when you recall your most positive consumer experiences—how it felt to receive great service— chances are, you think of the *person,* not the product.

Remember an individual who treated you

especially well, singled you out, and made the entire transaction pleasant and memorable. *You* are that person to your customers; you are the one they will remember. You understand the power of a smile and how one's friendly, helpful manner leaves a positive, lasting impression.

The secret in service is *people,* and that means you. Selling or serving customers well is simply a matter of putting what you know into practice. And it's no secret that the more you practice, the easier it gets!

Customers remember people over products. The real secret to service is you!

—C. Leslie Charles

2.

The "I's" Have It

Service: it's your job. Here are six facets of service that can help you better understand its unique nature and how you fit into the picture.

First, service is an **Intangible**. Unlike a product, it cannot be manufactured: service involves feelings and perceptions. The second unique aspect of service is its **Immediacy**. You have to be ready, willing, and able when your customer calls, walks through the door, or contacts you, regardless of whatever else is happening at the moment.

Service is **Invisible**. It's transparent—until things go wrong, that is. When a problem occurs, service becomes highly visible, especially to the customer; creating a perfect opportunity for you to shine! Service is also an **Interpersonal** transaction, requiring excellent communication, empathy, and listening skills.

You need to be polite, diplomatic, and sometimes gently firm, yet always courteous and professional.

Additionally, service is an **Individual** effort. Your customers think *you* are your organization. That's quite a responsibility, isn't it! And, last but not least, service is **Indelible**. Customers will remember for a long time how you treated them, and this determines whether or not they will return.

The point? Keep the **"I"** in your service: be friendly, responsive, precise, personable, responsible, *and* remembered!

> *You are extremely important— you put the the "I" in service.*
>
> —C. Leslie Charles

3.

Attitude Equals Service

Think about a time when you, as a customer, received exceptional service or sales. Chances are, the person serving you had a great attitude and helping you seemed like the most natural thing in the world. You walked away feeling really great because this employee was 100% "there" for you. Do your customers feel that way about you?

Service, just like life, begins with attitude. It's an 80/20 proposition, consisting of 80% attitude and 20% technique. If you have a positive attitude, the appropriate behaviors will naturally follow. With the right attitude, the right words will come out of your mouth, even if you're facing an upset customer.

Regardless of the circumstance, it pays to emphasize the positive. Here's an example: only about 20% of your customers will give you a tough time—

6

so why let such a small percentage of your customers ruin a large part of your day?

Positive thinking is actually a skill, and if you work on it every day, it will become a habit. At work or home, your positive attitude can transform problems into challenges, and obstacles into opportunities 100% of the time! Yes, the right attitude means successful service for you—and your customers—every time.

Customer service is 80% attitude and 20% technique: 80 + 20 equals 100% service!

—C. Leslie Charles

Service: What's in It for You?

The steps in giving good service are so simple anyone can quickly list them: smile, be courteous and friendly, respond promptly, know your job, answer questions, and follow up. Pretty basic.

Yet you've seen people who forget the basics when working with customers. They're indifferent, uncaring, uninterested. These employees don't realize what they sacrifice when they hold back on service, for giving good service has both external and internal rewards. The benefits go far beyond a paycheck.

Here's what I mean: taking your work seriously means wanting to do a good job. When you feel good about your work, you feel good about yourself. Not only does the act of giving good service help you feel better about yourself but when you treat others well, they usually respond in kind. You get treated well, too!

When your service is excellent you stand out among your peers: this can enhance your career possibilities. Organizations often reward, retain, and highly regard employees who excel in service. And service skills transfer from one job to another: they are never out of date!

Your customers benefit from good service and you benefit, too. Service is one of those situations where you get back what you give out—how could you ever want to give anything less than your absolute best?

Service skills are easy to identify, hard to practice, and impossible to do without.

—C. Leslie Charles

5.

People First, Paper Second

How many times have you requested information from a sales or service representative, only to have them hand you a piece of paper instead of offering a face-to-face explanation? Were you disappointed? Were you looking for a friendly exchange instead of a flyer in your hand? Here is a simple, yet powerful customer service secret: *people first, paper second.*

It helps to remember that service and sales involve building relationships. Paper can wait, but people won't. If customers are too quickly presented with, "What is your account number?" or "Do you have any insurance?" or "Here, this brochure explains…" they may just walk out the door.

You retain customers by building positive, long-term relationships, and customers remain loyal when they believe there is something in it for them. So get them invested. When your customers feel as if they share some kind of special relationship with you, they will be more likely to return.

Yes, you can actually be too quick to offer information—even answers. Just remember to take a moment and establish a *relationship* before you address the customer's request. Putting people first and paper second will help your customers think of you first—every time!

Service works best when you put people's needs first and paperwork needs second.

—C. Leslie Charles

6.

Who Cares?

You may have heard the old joke: "How do you feel about ignorance and apathy?" Answer: "I don't know and I don't care!"

As a customer, you've probably run into these types and it's no laughing matter: you've endured entire transactions with no eye contact, no smile, and no acknowledgment of your presence except when the person took payment for your merchandise.

Were you disappointed or irritated by their uncaring attitude? Did you decide they had just lost your business? Indifference is a losing proposition for both the customer and the employee—here's why.

Over time, our mood patterns become unconscious habits; a way of life. Workers who disconnect from their emotions systematically dull their senses; the indifference they practice eight hours a day becomes an ingrained way of living. They're bored and boring, but they don't have a clue what's wrong.

They are unaware that work performance is connected to personal performance and that how we behave at work is often how we behave at home.

Maybe these thoughts will help you remember that caring about the work you do is actually a way of caring about yourself. In the future, if someone ever asks, "Who cares?" you can say, "I do!" and really mean it.

How much you care will always show above and beyond how much you know.

—C. Leslie Charles

7.

Fake It Till You Make It

A smile is universally understood throughout the world, and it's essential to good service. You've probably been told that a smile can even be "heard" over the telephone, and it's true. On the phone or face to face, your smile sets the tone. If you want to be treated well by your customers and coworkers, smile more. A smile on your face sets positive expectations.

Of course, you may be thinking that it's easy to smile on a good day, but how about those times when you really don't feel like it? Guess what—smile anyway! That's right; a bad day is the best of all times to practice the old "fake it till you make it."

You are probably aware that how you feel on the inside affects how you look on the outside, but there's more. How you *look* also affects how you feel. That's right: smiling actually helps you feel better! As strange

The Customer Service Companion . . .

as it may seem, even a "fake" smile positively influences your mood. Just putting your facial muscles into a smile position will boost your energy level, relax you, and improve your mood. Try it and see!

Now, you may be concerned that forcing a smile is insincere, but don't worry about that. I'll be the first to admit that as a customer, I'd rather be waited on by someone who is *working* on a smile than someone who is being a 100% sincere, heartfelt grouch! How about you?

A smile looks great from both angles: looking at, or looking out.

—C. Leslie Charles

8.

An Ounce of Prevention

Every day, in every workplace, employees are interrupted by customers who are confused by poorly placed or nonexistent signs, inconvenient service delivery systems, unclear procedures, or faulty office layout. Here are two examples.

In a state government office where business owners must log onto a computer before filing business documentation, employees are continually interrupted with questions about how to use the computers. Why? Because when a user sits down at the keyboard, the posted instructions are no longer visible, yet no one in that office has taken the time to move the instruction sheet!

In another building, customers walk into a lobby to make a payment. The sign at the cashier window states "Payments Only," yet the cashier is constantly asked for directions because there is no building directory in the lobby. Customers are irritated by the lack of information and the poor cashier resents these all too frequent interruptions.

There are simple and obvious solutions to these problems. And there's a good lesson, too: rather than trying to live with irritating, unnecessary interruptions that frustrate your customers and prevent you from doing your job, *eliminate* them. Preventive planning is one small aspect of service that will make a big difference for everyone!

> *Rather than simply tolerating unnecessary interruptions, find a way to prevent them.*
>
> —C. Leslie Charles

9.

Special Delivery

Each organization has its own service delivery systems: some are designed with the customer in mind and some are not. As a customer, you've probably noticed that some organizations are a breeze to deal with while others make you jump through hoops.

Years ago, before the deregulation of the telecommunications industry, I visited a friend in Texas. In a field behind his house sat an old abandoned car sporting a faded bumper sticker with a telephone company logo. It read, "We don't care—we don't have to." An apt sign of the times.

It's a different world today: competition is fierce in every marketplace. Companies can no longer afford to behave as if they're the only game in town; they must adapt to customer needs. And delivery systems (how customers are served) need to be continually analyzed and adjusted.

How long has it been since your sales or service team assessed your systems? You need to regularly review your service structure, from initial impressions to the end of the transaction, to check the level of customer convenience. It's easy. Simply identify who the system truly serves—the customer or the company.

Are your procedures and systems designed for customer convenience or company convenience? If you're unsure, just ask your customers—they'll be happy to let you know!

Do your delivery systems serve your customers or do they serve your organization?

—C. Leslie Charles

10.

Service Works—Inside and Out

Customers are here, there, and everywhere. They are the lifeblood of any organization. If you happen to be reading this during a work break, look around. The people you see are your customers. Now, maybe you only see coworkers. In fact, maybe that's all you ever see: you may work "in the back" and seldom come in contact with the public.

But customers don't all come from the outside, they exist on the inside, too. This includes your manager and coworkers; even people from other departments. If you're a supervisor, your employees are your customers, and so is your manager. Put simply, a customer is someone who needs something from you, whether from the outside or inside.

One might think that good customer service begins externally, with public image and reputation, but it's actually the other way around. Internal service is where it starts. If people on the inside aren't treated well, and if they don't treat each other well, how could they possibly offer good service or sales to those on the outside?

How an organization treats its own naturally transfers to outsiders, and your own experiences as a customer bear this out.

Where you've been treated well is where employees are treated well. In short, customer service works from the inside out.

Customer service begins on the inside and works its way to the outside, not the other way around.

—C. Leslie Charles

A Matter of Time

Would you like your work time to go faster? Here's a tip: pay *full* attention to what you're doing and how you're doing it. Focus on the work that needs to be done, concentrate on helping your customers, and maintain a positive attitude. It makes a difference!

Years ago, when I had a bad attitude toward my job, I perfected the self-defeating practice of clock watching. I foolishly focused on the passing of time instead of my work. As a result, each hour crawled by. My mind was everywhere but in the present moment.

Today, I know that watching the clock distracts us from whatever is happening in the here and now. The sales and service employees who stay "in the moment" occupy themselves with what is happening in real time. They couldn't tell you if five or fifteen minutes have passed. And because they're so immersed in their work, all of a sudden it's time to go home!

The major difference is focus: effective service people would rather focus on *this* moment and what they can accomplish *now* instead of watching the clock.

On the other hand, clock watchers invest their energy in the future, and they end up getting exactly what they're looking for: slow moving time.

Effective service professionals are too busy working to notice (or care) what time it is!

Time flies for the person having fun and it crawls for the person having none.

—C. Leslie Charles

Forcing a Smile

When a credit union manager urged a teller to smile while working with customers, the teller retorted, "You can't make me!" It's true. No employer can enforce a smile. But by refusing to cooperate, the teller missed out on numerous physical and emotional benefits.

Are you aware that smiling lowers blood pressure, releases muscular tension, increases metabolism, produces endorphins (pain killing hormones), and reduces stress? The teller who refused to smile might just be experiencing some personal problems and smiling could help offset the tension or worry. And this is a perfect example of the fact that the very people who most need to smile will resist doing so because it just doesn't feel "right."

On the days you feel like that, force yourself to

smile anyway. Not only will you receive the benefits listed above, but when you smile, most people will smile back. They'll also treat you better. This in itself will help you feel more like smiling!

The point? If you want a simple way to enhance relationships with coworkers and customers, smile more. Everyone around you will benefit, and so will you.

In this tense, impatient, world, you could probably use a friendly face; why not make it your own?

> *While no one can force you to smile, your smile can be a powerful force.*
>
> —C. Leslie Charles

Taking Your Work Home

We've established that there are numerous ways you personally benefit from providing excellent service: when you smile, you feel better; when you concentrate on your work, time goes faster; and when you treat others well, they tend to treat you well. Yet, there's even more.

Consider that we human beings are creatures of habit and any behaviors we consistently practice become second nature, whatever they are. What we consider "good customer service" involves specific behaviors you choose to consciously practice on a daily basis until they become unconscious and second nature for you.

And all of the service skills you practice at work will work for you at home as well. Your positive attitude, cooperation, willingness to listen, and ability to defuse conflict will help improve your personal relationships.

This makes service a win/win proposition: your customers win because you help make life easier for them. And you win by helping make things a little easier at home, too.

Service skills are essential skills, professionally and personally. They are simply good living skills; and the best part? You *get paid* to learn and practice them! This is one instance where you'll want to take your work home with you—every single day!

> *If you treat your family like customers and your customers like family, things tend to work out pretty well.*
>
> —C. Leslie Charles

14.

No Problem

If a customer has a problem, you have a problem. And when people have problems, they are quick to express their frustration or anger. Handling a customer's problem is part of your job, and you can make this less troublesome by handling their emotions objectively and effectively.

Maybe you already know how to neutralize people's anger or hostility by actively listening and responding to their problem rather than wasting time defending yourself or your organizational systems. And you might also know that only by listening carefully can you truly grasp how the situation looks and feels from the customer's perspective.

Service under pressure works when you attack the problem, not the person. Rather than letting a problem come between you and your customer, do what you can to view the situation through your customer's eyes. This way, both of you attack the *problem,* not each other. You, in effect, join forces rather than trying to force the issue.

Here's what doesn't work: perceiving upset customers as the problem, personalizing their emotional outbursts, or trying to make them wrong.

From now on, instead of taking sides, keep yourself and your customer on the same side. This will help you make problem solving more problem free!

When you share your customer's problem you double the odds of solving it.

—C. Leslie Charles

The Tip of the Iceberg

There's more to people than meets the eye. Take yourself for example: you're a complex individual with a unique history, personality, beliefs, values, and perceptions. The same applies to your customers and coworkers. Each human being is like an iceberg: there's always far more going on beneath the surface than what is visible.

For example, when a customer is upset, all you may see or hear are harsh words and tense or angry body language. But consider what lies beneath all that: unique experiences, perceptions, needs, wants, fears, insecurities, and an individual way of expressing frustration. You're observing the *result* of someone's emotional state but you don't know the exact reason *why* the person feels this way.

Remember this the next time you face an upset

person: instead of reacting to what you see and hear, try to discover the underlying problem—the feelings and perceptions that exist beneath the surface. Getting to the core of the issue will give you the best chance for a positive resolution.

When working with an angry or upset person, remember that what you see or hear is only the tip of the iceberg. By taking the time to bypass visible behaviors and address the underlying problem, you'll have a better chance of smoothing troubled waters for good.

People are like an iceberg; it's what lies beneath the surface that causes the behaviors we see and hear.

—C. Leslie Charles

Declaration of Independence

We say that one bad apple can spoil the whole bunch. Maybe in the past you've let a coworker's negative mood or a difficult customer's demands ruin your day. This doesn't have to happen because you are capable of operating independently of other people's moods or behavior. Are you aware of that? Just as we set a clock, we can also set (or reset) our own mood!

Yes, it takes some work, but there is no reason, other than the choice you make, why someone else should ruin your day. Why give anyone so much power over you? From the driver who cuts you off on the way to work, to an upset and demanding customer, complaining coworker, or negative supervisor, you can, with a bit of effort on your part, be less affected by others.

You and you alone are the one who decides what

mood you want to be in, or how you will respond to other people's behavior. The only way you can truly have a lousy day is by *making the choice* to do so.

A nice deep breath, a smile, and your sense of humor can disconnect you from negative influences. Remember: how you want to feel about things is your choice. Through the power of your mind you can focus on positives rather than negatives. Consider this your personal "declaration of emotional independence" at work and home.

People may try to spread their stress, but the only one who can ruin your day is—guess!

—C. Leslie Charles

17.

Full Service

Some people jokingly say, "This would be a great job if it weren't for the customers!" But good service and sales are no joking matter. Whether you are part time, full time, seasonal, in a support or leadership position, experienced, or brand new on the job, you are entrusted to serve your customers.

It begins with attitude. How you view your job affects how you treat your customers: it also affects your desire to learn about, and promote, your products and services. A great attitude transforms your work into more than just a job, which makes it less "work" for you. A positive attitude inspires a full commitment to serve and sell.

Can you imagine someone saying, "Well, I only need to be *half* as nice to my customers as everyone else because I only work part-time." No way!

When you have a full commitment to service, customer's phone calls are not interruptions; they are the reason you have a job! And customer's complaints are not irritations; they are feedback and suggestions.

Questions are service opportunities and objections are a chance to educate your customer about products or services. You get the point.

Part-time or full-time, satisfying customer needs is what your job is all about, and your commitment to serve makes it all work!

When you commit to making sales and service work, your job becomes less "work."

—C. Leslie Charles

18

When Being Right is the Wrong Move

Although we say, "The customer is always right," we know this isn't true. And we also know that even when customers are in the wrong they don't want to admit it. In fact, the more wrong a customer is, the more insistent he or she may be. You must be prepared to listen, and in some cases, be lenient; a small concession on your part can save the day.

The first step is to hold your ego in tow. This is critical; ego often drives us to prove other people wrong. But you have nothing to gain and much to lose by making your customer wrong. If you can swallow your pride, smile in spite of your frustration, and attempt to please (or even appease), you will increase your chances of achieving positive results.

You reduce conflict by tactfully avoiding the issue of who is right and who is wrong. Instead, you can put your energy into solving the problem in a positive way.

The skills you practice to retain a customer may help you retain your job: the more customers there are, the more necessary you are.

So the next time you face an upset or angry customer, ask yourself: "Do I want to be right—or do I want results?" This will help you perceive the situation as a chance to create a positive outcome from an initially negative situation.

While your customers may not always be right, you always want to do right by them.

—C. Leslie Charles

19

Counting What Really Counts

Have you ever noticed that when we're having a bad day we tend to keep track of it, counting every irritation or inconvenience that occurs. You've heard the familiar complaint, "This is the third time today something lousy has happened!"

And while this may be a natural reaction, seldom, on a good day, do we exclaim, "This is the third time today something great has happened!"

So why do we keep track of the negatives but not the positives? Counting bad incidents simply adds to our stress, so consider the benefits of tallying the *good* things instead. For example, you might discover that far more positive events occur than negative ones.

Keeping track of good experiences puts you in a better frame of mind, motivating you to help others feel more positive, too. This increases the chances of everyone having a better time; what a nice thought!

And you just might find yourself anticipating incidents to *celebrate* rather than anguishing over the next terrible thing that's certain to happen any moment now.

It's worth a try, isn't it? Just remember, you are the scorekeeper; it's up to you to make the good times count!

Irritations are what you find when you allow negatives to enter your mind.

—C. Leslie Charles

20.

A Matter of Choice

Customers choose to do business with you when they have a specific want or need. If you are a sales person, you can appreciate that someone has chosen your products or services over those of your competitors. If you serve in the nonprofit or public sector, your customers may have fewer choices, but they still have a need for your assistance.

How you go about meeting a customer's need is your personal choice. Every day, you make choices about how you want to feel, how you will treat others (and yourself), and what kind of day you will have. If you choose to perceive that you are having a lousy day and that people are mean and difficult, you'll end up stressed out. But by choosing to perceive difficult people or events as a *personal challenge,* you'll end up creating more positive outcomes.

Admittedly, a small percentage of your customers will be difficult to deal with; this is true in every business. But upset customers are *still* your customers, and by choosing to help them, by meeting their needs, not only do you contribute to your organization's success, you end up looking like a hero!

Your customers make the choice to do business with you. And you can choose to treat them so well that it's an easy choice for them to come back, again and again and again.

You don't choose your customers; they choose you!

—C. Leslie Charles

21.

Acceptance or Approval?

In work and life, we have our good days and bad days, triumphs and challenges, adventures and embarrassments, joy and pain. We can learn from these different experiences if we so choose. Yet for some of us, our biggest lesson in life might be learning how to decrease our personal stress and increase our satisfaction level, regardless of the circumstance.

For example, you cannot control how others treat you, but you can control your own behavior. Yes, things will happen that you won't like, or that you cannot change, undo, or redo. This can be hard to accept. But acceptance and approval are two separate issues: you can come to *accept* even a painful situation, without ever having to approve of it.

Understanding the difference between acceptance and approval can make it easier for you to withstand a customer's unjustified tirade, a lost sale, an unfair performance review, or an organizational change you consider less than ideal.

The capability of separating acceptance from approval might help you adjust to an unfortunate circumstance in your own life, or that of a loved one.

The bad news is, you cannot change the world nor the people in it, but the good news is, that accepting this hard truth can relieve some of your stress immediately.

You cannot control everything that happens to you, but you can control how you respond to it.

—C. Leslie Charles

22.

What's in a Name?

In presenting my customer service seminars to both corporate and public sector clients, the question "what do you call your customers?" often comes up. In most for-profit organizations, the word customer is common, but an HMO, insurance plan, or credit union has subscribers or members. In hospitality, the words guest or patron might apply, while hospitals, clinics, medical and dental offices, or veterinary practices typically work with patients or clients.

But in law enforcement or government regulatory agencies, is the person who is cited for a violation truly a *customer?* In one session we explored alternative words: citizen, client, constituent, taxpayer, other party, or employer. Although some people may say it doesn't make any difference, what you call your customers does reflect your perceptions of them.

And how you *perceive* your customers influences how you treat them. It also affects how they perceive and treat you, too.

If there is any question in your organization about the best word for your customers, discuss it. Be sure to choose something that both fits your function and denotes some level of appreciation or respect.

For regardless of the nature of your business, it's your customers who keep you in business!

> *What you call your customers will affect how you treat them, and how you treat your customers will affect how they treat you.*
>
> —C. Leslie Charles

23

About Face

You know that smiling helps you look friendly and approachable to a customer; it can create a positive first impression and help put others at ease, but there's more. The smile on your face can also help put *you* at ease, too.

A group of researchers recently investigated the connection between one's facial expression and emotional state. Participants were given instructions which, when followed, created the facial expressions commonly associated with emotions such as fear, suspicion, happiness, sadness, and so on.

Subjects were asked to position their mouth, eyes, eyebrows, and forehead in ways that represented these emotions but the exercise was strictly objective: no reference was made about feelings or mental state.

Yet when participants were asked to describe

their emotional reactions following the experiment, their comments reflected the expressions they had worn.

Individuals whose faces *looked* happy or positive reported feeling that way during the project. Those whose faces *looked* unhappy or negative felt edgy or uncomfortable. So what's the point?

Even if you're having a rough day, smile. Sooner or later, your smile will rub off on the person you most want to influence—yourself!

> *If you're having a good day, let your face know— because how your face looks reflects how life looks to you.*
>
> —C. Leslie Charles

24

Making Sense of Humor

Our funniest stories often reflect our most painful, embarrassing or stressful experiences, yet in the retelling they seem hysterical and humorous. Let's face it; humor keeps us nimble. With a good sense of humor you can roll with the punches, rebound after a bad experience, or release your tension in the midst of a harried, high pressure day.

My two most memorable audiences were health care insurance company employees who spend their work day answering questions, listening to complaints, solving billing problems, or clarifying company policy for subscribers. High pressure work, but these people know the best way to relieve stress is with a smile.

Do they laugh at their customers? No, they laugh at themselves. They have learned to look on the lighter side of a stressful job, and it works!

While work is serious business, we all need to take ourselves a bit less seriously. If you haven't been laughing much lately, if your office is a somber place, see what you and your coworkers can do to lighten it up.

By engaging your sense of humor, your work day will seem shorter and your mental fuse will be longer. It's your number one stress management tool.

When you teach yourself to lighten up and laugh off your work stress, you'll feel a lot more like living it up after hours!

It always makes good sense to exercise your sense of humor.

—C. Leslie Charles

25

What Did You Expect?

We've all heard that we tend to get back from people what we expect from them; here's an example. At one time, a friend's husband was a pretty glum guy. When she encouraged him to warm up, he snapped, "Why should I be friendly—no one is friendly to me!"

She explained that the reason people weren't very friendly to him was because of his negative expectations. The look on his face and his gruff manner put people off; they backed away or withdrew because he appeared so unfriendly.

After much discussion he grudgingly agreed to a week of experimenting with a more positive approach. Within three days he was amazed at all of the friendly faces he came across—in his whole life he had never seen so many warm, positive people!

He learned that his negative expectations and the

corresponding look on his face put people off before they ever had a chance to get acquainted with him.

What are your expectations of customers and coworkers? Do you anticipate friendly treatment and cooperation from others? Or competition and resistance? Maybe your outlook, and the look on your face, are prompting others to give you exactly what you expect.

Here's hoping you have high expectations!

Expect the best: always be on the lookout for a positive outlook.

—C. Leslie Charles

26.

A Telling Subject

There are some service and sales people who just don't seem to get it. These unmotivated individuals send out all kinds of negative messages without even realizing it; unconsciously broadcasting to customers in various ways that they really aren't too fired up about their job. How? With the most powerful form of communication: body language.

You've seen it all from such employees yourself. A lack of eye contact, a deep sigh, a frown, a look of terminal boredom or a personal phone call throughout an entire interaction. A "tsk" or smirk, a shrug or a casual toss of a hand in a general direction rather than personally accompanying customers to the location they're trying to find. These unconscious behaviors are a loud and clear statement of personal indifference and professional incompetence.

Worst of all, these employees are clueless about the undermining effects of their poor attitude. For them, work is boring and no fun. And because they are bored, they're also boring; it's not a whole lot of fun working with them.

Let their silent language be a telling lesson for the rest of us that attitude always comes through loud and clear. Unfortunately, the recipient gets the message, but the sender doesn't. Maybe some day someone will tell them.

Our body language has a lot to say about us.

—C. Leslie Charles

27.

For Rent

Several years ago while traveling, I struck up a conversation with a woman. When I asked what she did for a living, she replied, "I'm a Customer Service Representative for the Royal Bank of Canada." I was preparing for a series of bank-related customer service seminars so I began asking about her job.

It was immediately evident that she had an unusually positive attitude about her work, especially when she said that dealing with difficult customers or coworkers was no problem; in fact, she enjoyed it.

Catching the amazement on my face, she laughed and said, "Here's my attitude: the bank rents me from 8 to 5. And while I'm being rented I'm expected to serve my customers and coworkers to the best of my ability, regardless of their behavior."

She added, "When 5:00 comes and I'm dealing

with a problem, I remind myself that this is a 'rented' problem and I leave it at work. I also try to leave my personal problems at home where they belong. It all works out pretty well."

I've remembered her story vividly all this time. How do you handle things while you're being rented? And do people remember *you* for years and years?

There are all kinds of ways to say, "I'm just doing my job." The best way to say it is with a smile.

—C. Leslie Charles

28.

A Place for Everything

Okay, let's face it; there are good days and bad days. We all have them. The hard part about customer service is that you're never supposed to have a bad day, or when you do, you're expected to keep it a secret from your customers.

This gets complicated because you actually have two kinds of customers; external and internal ones. Chances are, your internal customers (coworkers) know you well enough that they can tell what kind of day you're having and some of them will empathize. But your external customers don't know, nor do they care, if you're having a bad day. They just want friendly, competent service, regardless.

You can help yourself handle the bad days better by learning how to *compartmentalize.* The skill of compartmentalizing allows you to temporarily place your frustration or bad mood in a mental "drawer" and let it stay out of sight. You tell yourself, "I'll deal with this later, when it's more appropriate."

By allowing yourself to compartmentalize, you avoid letting a bad mood get in the way of your work. This is how skilled athletes learn to perform under pressure, and you can do it, too.

You can focus your energy on things that need to be done instead of feeling as if things are being done to you. You'll benefit from this handy skill, and so will everyone around you!

If you're having a bad day, the last person who wants or needs to know is your customer.

—C. Leslie Charles

29.

Sales is Service, Service is Sales

Sales is often defined as the skillful transfer of enthusiasm from one person to another. That's exactly what service is, too. Sales involves service and service involves sales, even when there isn't a tangible product involved. That's because, in both cases, the first thing you are selling is yourself.

Some people tell me, "But I'm not a sales person—I'm a natural at serving, but I *hate* selling!" We then discuss that while doing business involves an exchange of various products, services, or resources, the one consistent, central component in all of these examples is people. You simply can't do business without customers! While technology may help us increase our efficiency and improve our systems, people are always essential to the process. And you are a big part of that.

Whether you work in sales, service, or both, your customers need to be sold on *you*. Customers remember how they are treated, and if you do your best to meet their needs and requests, you are selling, whether you know it or not.

Here's how you can simplify the sales process: just do what's appropriate for your customers, do your best to meet their needs, and you'll be doing your job. Sales is service and service is sales. It's the most natural combination in the world.

When you're sold on service, you're sold on sales, and this means your customers are sold on you.

—C. Leslie Charles

30.

All Clear

If the world were perfect, we'd never have to deal with upset customers or unreasonable demands. But alas, part of your job involves listening to feedback, criticism, complaints, and objections: you may even get yelled at from time to time. Of course, there are limits to the abuse you must tolerate, and you need to discuss this with your supervisor.

Departmental policies can help protect you from extreme or unacceptable behaviors. But you also need emotional protection from these encounters: a quick way of recovering from stressful interactions so you can get back to work and still feel good about yourself.

Simply *hear it* and *clear it*. It's your special "emotional immune system" where the negative stuff just doesn't take. You listen as the customer ventilates, you empathize and do everything you can to solve the problem, and then you let it go. The better your ability to hear it and clear it, the easier your job will be.

Customers yell and vent frustration because they feel a situation is out of control. They often recognize that it's not your fault, but still feel compelled to yell anyway. So the next time someone gets upset, remind yourself to hear it and clear it. See what a difference it can make!

After dealing with an upset customer, I can "hear it and clear it" from my mind, and leave the negative incident behind.

—C. Leslie Charles

31

First Impressions Last

Prompt acknowledgment is the first step in customer service. Even if you cannot immediately wait on someone, at least smile or nod to create a positive first impression.

I once checked into a hotel with six people behind the desk (one of whom was the manager). Only two employees were checking in guests; the other four were occupied with a problem while a customer waited, totally ignored, for five minutes. By the time someone finally helped him, the man was understandably upset. One of the clerks could have at least acknowledged his presence or explained why he was having to wait.

Think of this guest's first impression of the hotel. Even if his room was delightful, meals excellent, and the checkout flawless, he will most likely remember his initial experience of having to wait. And wait.

First impressions are critical: always begin with a friendly acknowledgment. Connect with customers through eye contact and a smile: they will immediately feel good about doing business with you.

If there will be a wait, promptly explain *why* rather than making your customer guess. Do whatever you can to create positive first impressions, because chances are, they will last— for a long, long time!

First impressions are lasting impressions.

—C. Leslie Charles

32.

The Hidden Me

As a child, did you enjoy the game of finding the hidden animals in a picture, or discovering how many little words you could find in a big one? Here's a customer service spin on that game: there are two critical hidden words in *customer* and they are both essential to giving good service.

Of course, the first word is *us*. Teaming up; working with your customer is the first step in service. The second essential word is *me*. Every customer is unique in some way; there is a special *me* hidden inside, and your job is to figure out what each of your customers want from you. By searching for the *me* inside each customer, you'll discover how each individual wants or expects to be treated.

Some want you to be friendly and courteous and some want you to educate or inform them. Others need you to listen: they need to vent their frustration or demonstrate to you how much they know. Some customers will want you to take extra time while others just want fast, efficient service. Some love the sales process, while others don't.

Team up with your customers so you can find their hidden *me*. This way, you'll quickly learn what they want or need from you. In this game, everybody wins!

Within every customer you see, do your best to find the hidden "me."

—C. Leslie Charles

33.

Mirror, Mirror, on the Wall

Every relationship we have, whether personal or professional, makes a statement about us. This is because different people bring out different aspects of our character and personality.

Think about good friends or coworkers you like and how you behave around them. Then consider those individuals you're not so crazy about, and how you act in their company. What do these dynamics say about you?

Evaluate your relationships with each of your customers; they bring out different sides of you, too. While you know you're supposed to treat all of your customers positively and professionally, some will be easier than others. Certain customers will bring out your best, and others will seem to bring out your worst.

You can learn more about your behavior by

viewing each customer as a special "mirror." Pay close attention as each person reacts to how you treat them.

Seeing the effects of your *actions* reflected through your customer's *reactions* just might change the way you see yourself. You can learn what works best with people and what doesn't work, as well.

This eye opening exercise helps you assess your behavior as it gets mirrored back to you. You get a quick look at how you look—from someone else's unique point of view!

> *Every customer is like a special mirror, reflecting something in yourself you might not otherwise see.*
>
> —C. Leslie Charles

34

Letting Go of "No"

Regardless of how positive or helpful you want to be, there will be times when you have to say no or somehow disappoint a customer. This is a fact of life. Just remember that it isn't always what you say, it's how you say it.

In service it's important to send positive signals to your customers (as in, "yes, I want to help you" or "yes, I will do my best to assist you") but there will be times when you must say no. You can take comfort in knowing there are ways to say no positively, and good reasons for doing so, too.

When you are the customer, consider how much you dislike being told "We can't do that" or "It's against policy." It's the same for your customers. If you want to deliver consistently positive sales and service, you will want to reduce your use of the words, *no, not, don't* and *can't*. They are like slamming a door in your customer's face.

Instead of saying "I can't do that," try "I am unable to do that…" or "We are prohibited from doing that…" If you then add, "Here's what we *can* do…" you've done your best to keep the door open while cushioning "the blow of saying no."

Whenever possible, do what you can to emphasize the positive. Your ability to let go of "no" shows that when it comes to service, you are "in the know."

Even negatives can be delivered in a positive way.

—C. Leslie Charles

35.

Staying in Touch

There will be times when you are unable to immediately solve a customer's problem. You may have to wait for special information or instructions, talk with other people, or search long and hard for a solution. But while you are doggedly pursuing an answer or option, your customers will have no idea of what is going on unless you let them know.

The longer customers have to wait for a response from you, the more unsure they become: without feedback they have no idea of how hard you are working to help them. In the absence of updates, they begin thinking you've forgotten all about them. To avoid this, stay in touch with your customers, even if you have nothing new to report.

So rather than waiting until you have a complete answer or solution, make a quick call, or even a series of calls. Your brief progress reports will be appreciated. Telling your customer, "I still don't know anything for sure, but I'm working on it." is far superior to silence.

Take the initiative and let customers know their problem is still uppermost in your mind. To the customer, no news is bad news; they'll think you've forgotten them. A quick note or call is all it takes. Your customers will feel better, and you will look better in their eyes.

Staying in touch with customers adds a special touch to your service!

—C. Leslie Charles

36

Hold That Line

The telephone is an important service and sales tool and you know that customers will call at their convenience, not yours. Sometimes a ringing phone seems like an interruption but even if it's your fortieth call of the day, remember—it is the caller's first!

Telephone communication is unique: unlike face-to-face interactions, you cannot touch or see what is happening with the other party; nonverbal channels are missing. Your voice tone, pacing, and ability to listen are your only communication modes.

To truly connect, you need to immediately get—and stay—on the caller's wave length. Here's how: always answer as soon as possible, preferably by the second ring, and keep a pencil and pad handy for notes. Smile, it relaxes your vocal chords.

Give the caller your full attention and do your

best to sound friendly and unhurried. Listen carefully. Write down the person's name and other essential information.

Be patient. "Pace" yourself with the caller's rhythm: establish rapport by letting your behavior slightly reflect the caller's volume, speed, or mood (except, of course, when they are mad!).

Last but not least, let the caller hang up first. Remove the receiver from your ear, hesitate for a second or two, then gently hang up. These tips will help you connect every time!

Anytime you're on the phone, your skills are truly on the line.

—*C. Leslie Charles*

37

Taking Things into Account

In school we learned the "three R's:" reading, writing, and arithmetic. But there's one "R" we weren't taught: relationships. Your world revolves around relationships at work and home and here's a way you can evaluate how well they are working.

Think of relationships as dynamic and ever changing rather than static or fixed. Consider that a relationship is either strengthened or weakened with every contact; few interactions are neutral. You could regard your relationships as a series of emotional bank accounts in which deposits or withdrawals are continually being made. Of course, a positive interchange represents a deposit and a negative or strained encounter a withdrawal.

When a customer transaction ends, you can, with a bit of reflection, immediately determine if it was a plus or minus. You can even identify what you might do the next time to help your customers feel better about doing business with you.

Keep yourself focused on the aspect of adding something extra to your relationships rather than taking something away. By making each interaction a *plus* rather than a minus, every relationship can give you a significant return on your investment.

> When your customers walk away—make sure you added something to their day.
>
> —C. Leslie Charles

38.

No Bad News

While customers don't always notice when sales and service go well, they quickly spot mistakes, and sometimes their remarks are right on target. Listen to customer feedback. Legitimate complaints and constructive criticism help you make improvements, so respond to them promptly and professionally.

A customer's criticism may initially sound like bad news yet, in truth, it's just the opposite. How you *handle* mistakes, difficulties, or complaints can make you (and your organization) look great. Complaints are a mixed bag, but whether a customer is expressing some well-deserved criticism or simply having a bad day, do your best to help him or her feel better.

It doesn't take a lot, and you can make a big difference by listening, agreeing with whatever part of the complaint is accurate, and working through the problem together.

Keep in mind that whenever you help an upset customer feel good, you end up looking good. And when you change a system based on customer feedback, your organization looks good.

When you perceive complaints as opportunities, the good news will always outweigh the bad. Your efforts to listen and respond help make and keep a loyal customer. From now on, think of a complaining customer as a special *opportunity* for you to excel!

Some customers never complain, but they may never return either.

—C. Leslie Charles

39.

A Matter of Style

In service and sales we like to think that the golden rule works, but this isn't always true. People want to be treated *their* way rather than our way. If you pay close attention to customers and coworkers you'll be able to read their cues and clues.

Perceptive service and sales professionals know how to treat customers as they want to be treated. For example, some customers are upbeat and positive, even in stressful situations, and they prefer that you follow suit. Their smile or friendliness are clues.

On the other hand, a lighthearted manner might be perceived as uncaring by a customer who is in a more serious mood. Knowing how to appropriately adapt to people's styles will make your sales and service exceptional.

How can you do this? Pay attention. Read facial

expressions and voice tones. Look and listen. Observe people's energy levels: are they fast paced, moderate, or laid back? Read their moods: are they serious or playful, rushed or relaxed? Note their attitudes: are they happy, harried, or hostile? Follow their cues.

Your ability to *style flex* (adapt to, and act on what you observe) puts you in a unique category as a communicator. It will add a personal touch as you sell and serve your customers.

Serving others well serves you well.

—C. Leslie Charles

40.

An Inside Job

Do you ever look at your workplace from the eye of your customers? Tomorrow when you go to work, pretend you're a visitor. From the driveway to the parking lot, from the sidewalk to the front door, from the entry way to the lobby or waiting area, from the elevator or stairway to the rest room, from your office to your desk or work station, try to experience everything as a new customer would.

What are your first impressions? What do you see, hear, feel, smell, experience? What needs to be cleaned, repaired, painted, or made more visually appealing? How prominent and clear are the signs? If you were to call, would the person answering the phone enunciate and take a message cordially and correctly? If one were to have any kind of physical disability, how accessible is your place of business?

Customer service is a series of distinct experiences and interactions. How often might your customers be inconvenienced by existing systems, structures, or procedures? How long must they wait to be served? Are customers exposed to employee conversations in the cafeteria, stairwells, waiting areas, or elevators?

Determine if people's first and last impressions will be favorable or negative. Once you view things from the outside in, you've got the inside scoop on what it takes to please a customer!

Look at your workplace from your customer's eyes and you might just be in for a big surprise.

—C. Leslie Charles

41

You Serve When You Sell

Some employees say they want to *serve* their customers, not sell them. They think selling means being overbearing or pushy, but sales and service go together: if you're not selling a product, you're selling a service. And you are always selling yourself!

If you work in a sales culture, your customers need your products. Sales is simply a case of knowing what you have to offer, understanding what your customers need, and finding the proper fit between the two. If you let customers know how your products or services can help meet their need, you have served your customers well.

Some sales people say they are uncomfortable probing and asking questions because they don't want to appear nosy. But the questions you ask are simply ways of showing interest in your customers.

Most of them will appreciate this, especially if you begin with the words what and how (rather than why): "What exactly were you looking for…" "What additional needs might you have in the near future…" "How did this product work for you before…" or "How was it that this item didn't work for you…"

A service attitude helps you sell. Enjoy the process of getting to know your products and services, getting to know your customer's needs, and making the best match between the two.

Good service people need to be good sales people, and vice versa.

—C. Leslie Charles

42

The Power of Choice

Choice is a powerful thing. You have the power to choose how you treat others; to choose whether you will have a good day or bad day. And you exercise this power continually—with your customers, coworkers, manager, and even your loved ones. Regardless of how other people treat you, you are always in charge of how you act and react. If you pay attention to what you are thinking and feeling, and if you choose your actions carefully, you'll be amazed at the results.

Speaking of choice, providing great sales and service is a personal choice, regardless of the situation. Even in stressful times you can choose to focus on the positive aspects, no matter how small or insignificant they may seem. Behavior is a choice, and there is power in making positive choices. Your attitude is a choice, too. Resist "catching" the negative mood of a coworker or customer; this is how you give your power away. Refuse to be brought down by negative people; remind yourself that you *do* have a choice in the matter!

Exercising the power of choice both guarantees great service and surpasses the scope of the workplace. These ideas apply to every aspect of your life.

By choosing to serve others well, you serve your own well-being. What could be more powerful than that?

You have the power to choose how you will think, feel, and act, both at work and at home.

—*C. Leslie Charles*

43

Minimum Wage

There's an old joke about a person touring a company who asks, "How many people work here?" The answer: "About half of 'em!" This raises a good question: what if we were compensated, not for the hours we actually worked, but for the actual effort we expended? What if only giving minimum effort meant getting minimum salary?

You've probably worked with people who avoided doing anything extra: those who waited to be told what had to be done. That you are reading this book means you are more than a minimalist: you're willing to pull your fair share and then some. Those who use excuses such as, "That's not my job" or "I didn't notice" are frustrating to work with. They won't go out of their way for any reason.

We all know, deep inside, when we are doing a

good job and when we aren't. By holding back, we cheat ourselves out of the creativity, enjoyment, and enthusiasm of achievement.

What happens when you give just a little bit more than expected? You gain the personal satisfaction of knowing you did your best. Your manager or customers will be favorably impressed and you'll feel good about yourself.

By giving maximum effort you'll gain maximum personal reward: a sense of pride in your work. Now who could put a dollar figure on that?

Doing just a little bit extra can pay off big for you.

—*C. Leslie Charles*

44

Send Me the Tough Ones

Let's be realistic: dealing with unhappy and upset people is an important part of your job. While it's no fun handling an upset customer, consider the one positive element—the complaining customer is *still* your customer—at least for now!

You see, a large percentage of dissatisfied customers simply walk away without a word. They never give anyone a second chance to make things right. This means your upset customers are actually *opportunities,* for they are giving you another chance to regain their trust.

Years ago, one of my seminar attendees stated that she loved dealing with upset people. She smiled and declared, "Send me the tough ones!" And she meant it. This woman delighted in helping upset people feel better and it was her positive attitude that made the difference.

With the right attitude, you, too, can handle the tough ones: if a customer is upset, find out what is wrong and why. Do your best to help people calm down; listen to them carefully, and consider their feelings, even if they aren't considering yours at the moment. Fix their problem and they'll stick with you through thick and thin.

Handling upset people is a skill; something you can excel in, if you have the right attitude. Just view it as an opportunity, not an obstacle.

> *Be tough on problem solving and tender with people.*
>
> —C. Leslie Charles

45

Spreading the Word

People often say that moods are "contagious" or "infectious." Would you agree? How often are you affected by someone's good (or bad) mood? Because mood transmission is a highly unconscious process, we can all benefit by becoming more aware of how we influence, or are influenced by others.

If moods are contagious, think about what you are passing on to others in the course of your work day: what moods do you "spread" when you come in contact with customers? You can pass on pleasure, pressure, stress, or a smile; the choice is yours.

Working in customer service or sales puts you in the "people" business. Consider what this means: tally up the number of individuals with whom you interact in the course of just one day, and you can measure the scope of your influence.

Who knows how many customers and coworkers will go away feeling more energized (or irritated) by your behavior? How many people will *they* come in contact with after being influenced by you?

Just think, your one act of kindness, friendly smile, or extra effort will ripple through untold numbers of people as a result. Consider it your job to spread the good word!

How we treat one person; what we do or say, can influence hundreds of people a day.

—C. Leslie Charles

Quick Fix

When it comes to service, you know there will always be problems, but you don't have to think of them as problems. When handled promptly and properly, a customer's problem can offer positive outcomes, especially if you approach the situation with the right attitude.

The critical component to effective problem solving is response time, so the minute a customer has a problem, make it yours. Immediately separate the person from the problem and commit your energy to finding a workable solution right now rather than trying to prove the customer wrong. Trying to attach blame only makes for bigger problems and you don't have time for that.

You will benefit by addressing all problems promptly, because the longer a customer has to live with a problem, the greater the chance it will get blown out of proportion.

The point? Attitude and timeliness are the secrets to success. A problem which gets addressed promptly and positively (even when it is only partially solved), usually pleases customers more than a long, drawn out solution.

Problem solving is one situation that operates on its own time frame—now!

The longer a customer has a problem the bigger it gets.

—C. Leslie Charles

47

All's Well That Ends Well

We discussed first impressions earlier in this book, but there needs to be a word on last impressions, too. Think of the parting moment with your customer as a last opportunity to create a favorable memory: a chance to apply your sales and service skills one last time.

Combine your smile, direct eye contact, helpful attitude, and good posture to create a pleasant parting memory. By helping your customers feel well served, you increase their chances of returning. But it isn't over until it's over: make those last minutes count!

Customers notice when you take the time to acknowledge them and they appreciate any attempt on your part to help them feel good about the services or products you provide, especially toward the end of your transaction.

If you are in sales and your customer makes a significant purchase, reinforce the sale by commenting on what a good decision they've made, or how much practical use they will get from this item. If the purchase was extravagant, tell them what a good investment it will be. Even a small purchase is worth commenting on.

Politeness, respect, a sincere *thank you* and a warm *good-bye* can make customers want to repeat the experience. Help them leave on a positive note.

A friendly farewell often means many happy returns.

—C. Leslie Charles

48.

Can You Spare Some Change?

As you read and reflect on the ideas and suggestions in this book, maybe you've thought about how tough it is to change a behavior, even when it's for the better.

Good habits are hard to begin and easy to break, and bad habits are easy to begin and hard to break. You can probably relate.

When you begin working on a new behavior, at first it will feel uncomfortable and unfamiliar. You may think, "This feels phony—it just isn't me!" You need to overcome this initial resistance before you can integrate new behaviors. It's only a matter of time.

It seems that attempting a change in attitude or behavior is similar to the organ transplant process: one immediately experiences a potential rejection period. But with the right kind of support, persistence, and determination, success is imminent. It's a case of try, try again.

You know what kind of person you want to be; you even have some ideas about how to do it. So in your attempts to improve your service or sales skills, be patient. Keep on trying. If you backslide, begin again. And again.

Positive persistence is how you make big changes happen, by taking one small step at a time.

Initiating a behavior change is similar to the organ transplant process: the hard part is getting over the initial rejection period.

—C. Leslie Charles

49

Turnabout is Fair Play

We've made the point that it pays to give great service, but let's remember that as a customer, you also *get* the best treatment by exercising your customer service skills. Here are a few hints on how to get the service you want and deserve.

Of course, the first thing is to smile. Service and sales people tend to respond more positively to someone who looks and acts friendly. Get people's full attention by helping break through the trance that often sets in with repetitive work. Employees may slip into auto pilot, but you can help them wake up again.

Say something special; give a compliment, or notice something about the employee or their work area that other customers miss. Engage service personnel in positive conversations. Energize them with your friendly manner and good mood.

My partner, Rob, is a master at this. People at the bank and post office are eager to wait on him. He even *tipped* our dental hygienist last year, and received a thank you note from her. She said this was her only tip in twelve years of practice, but she was one up on our dentist—he's never received one!

You'll be amazed at how you can turn a person's mood around by simply being an enthusiastic customer. And you're far more likely to get the great service you deserve. Try it!

> *You get the best service from others when you give them your best.*
>
> —C. Leslie Charles

50

A Lasting Thought

After my presentations, people often say, "I feel really motivated right now, but motivation doesn't last." Well, neither does a good meal!

We seem to think that one seminar, book, or speech should inspire us forever, but we need more than an occasional exposure. I hope you're enjoying *The Customer Service Companion* and that you'll keep it with you and let it be your daily motivator.

You see, every day we are exposed to negative attitudes, disturbing news reports, demanding people, and frustrating events. Just as our bodies need to be properly fed, so do our brains. We need to offer ourselves constant positive reinforcement to offset the many negative influences so prevalent in our society.

This book is a positive resource you can use on a daily basis. I encourage you to read it, or something

motivational, educational,
or inspirational every day.
If you drive more than ten
minutes to or from work,
consider playing educational
tapes in your car. Limit your
exposure to bad news and
negative information.
Practice positive self-talk.
And keep reading this book:
you'll discover different
ideas with every reading.

Keep a journal of your
ideas, goals, action steps,
and accomplishments. As
you know, the spirit of
service goes well beyond the
workplace, and I wish you
the best of service, both in
the giving and receiving!

*The spirit of
service is ongoing.
Let it be your
constant
companion.*

—C. Leslie Charles

notes

Quick Reminders
on
Customer Service

51.

Serving customers can sometimes be stressful, but having NO customers to serve can be even more so!

52.

When you put your customers first you build relationships that last.

53.

If you're having a bad day, keep it a secret. Most of the people you come in contact with don't want to know, and a few of them are having a worse day than you.

54.

Your best service tools are built in: your attitude, smile, positive words, friendly tone, and willingness to problem solve.

55.

You can't control other people's behavior but you can control your own.

56.

Service is 80% attitude and 20% technique.

The Customer Service Companion . . .

57.

Making things easier for your customers often makes things easier for you.

58.

To bring out the best in others, listen.
To bring out the best in yourself, listen.

59.

If you put your customer's needs first they'll be more likely to give you a second chance.

60.

Your sense of humor is your best stress management tool. If you can produce a smile you can reduce your stress.

61.

Here's a positive note about upset customers—they're giving you one more chance to keep their business!

62.

Make service a World Class event: just like an athlete, let your best come out whenever you face the worst of circumstances.

63.

How you treat other people always tells you something about yourself.

64.

Remember—upset customers have less to lose than you do.

65.

*Service is an exercise in personal leadership.
Look at the best leaders. They don't lead;
they serve!*

66.

*Do your best to enjoy your work time:
why would anyone choose to be
miserable that many hours of their life?*

67.

The service skills you practice at work will also work for you at home.

68.

Smile on the telephone—it relaxes your vocal chords and modulates your voice. You'll look better, and sound better, too!

69.

You have more power than you think: you can change the dynamics of a relationship if you are willing to change your behavior.

70.

When you are discussing a serious subject, keep your facial expression open and relaxed and your eyebrows in "neutral"—avoid frowning.

71.

Practicing good service means you will go home feeling good about yourself instead of bad about others.

72.

Even when customers are wrong, help them save face. Go for positive results instead of having to be "right."

73.

When a customer has a problem, you also have a problem: team up and solve the problem together.

74.

When there's a problem or conflict, do a quick attitude check. Are you trying to fix the problem or fix the blame?

75.

People first, paper second.

76.

People will tell you how they want you to treat them if you're willing to listen.

The Customer Service Companion . . .

77.

Consistent customer criticism and complaints are often a message that service systems need to be improved.

78.

Behavior is like an iceberg: get beneath the surface behaviors you see and hear to find out where the real problem lies.

79.

It pays to use positive words because whenever you speak, there are always two listeners: your customers and yourself!

80.

Whenever you begin feeling rushed, take a deep breath, relax, smile, and s-l-o-w down!

81.

Positive thinking does make a difference. Your thoughts affect your feelings and your feelings affect your behavior.

82.

If you're having a bad day, force yourself to treat people especially well. They'll end up treating you better, which means you'll end up feeling better.

83.

Smiling is a mental exercise. It's like doing pushups for your brain.

84.

Whether you have a good day or a bad day is up to you. Good service —and a good attitude—are your personal choice.

85.

When you focus on helping others with their problems you tend to forget about your own.

86.

Even when other people get upset, you don't have to. Someone needs to stay in charge, and you're better off if it's you!

87.

When you make a mistake, rather than treating it as a failure, consider it "education." Learn from it and move on.

88.

Solve customer problems promptly: the longer a person has a problem, the bigger it gets.

89.

When you consider how many hours you
spend with your coworkers, it makes sense
that you'd want to get along with them.

90.

When it comes to service, be positive.
Negative thinking is a magnifying
glass that makes problems huge
and possibilities small.

91.

Good intentions aren't enough. We may judge ourselves on our intentions but customers judge us on our performance.

92.

When you face grumpy customers, ask yourself how much kindness it will take to turn them around and go for it!

93.

You cannot not communicate; you are always sending silent messages to others. Make sure that the message you send is the one you intend!

94.

The stories satisfied customers tell about you and your organization are the best advertisements in the world, and they are free!

95.

If someone treats you poorly for a few moments, don't give them the satisfaction of letting it ruin your entire day.

96.

You have the capacity to transform customer service problems into challenges and sales obstacles into opportunities—
it's all in how you look at it.

97.

*Keep your ego out of the way when
working with customers. When your ego
is low, your empathy is high, and vice
versa. Only one works at a time.*

98.

*If you must work with someone you
dislike, don't let it get you down.
You only have to work with them,
not live with them!*

99.

Service is: building relationships, meeting customer needs, and creating a sense of satisfaction.

100.

Sales is: building relationships, meeting customer needs, and creating a sense of satisfaction.

101.

Always do what you can to ensure that when customers leave they feel better than when they walked in.

102.

There will be days when someone treats you badly. Let it go. Any resentment or thoughts of revenge on your part will end up hurting you, not them.

103.

Your smile is part of your work "uniform."
Wear it every day!

104.

When you strive to exceed customer
expectations, sometimes you exceed
your own.

105.

Cooperate with coworkers. Teamwork is the internal aspect of customer service, and your attitude helps make the team work!

106.

Be careful of your conversations with coworkers if you work in an area where customers are within earshot.

107.

The more you help others feel good about themselves, the better you will feel about yourself.

108.

In service, there are no small or unimportant jobs. Every job that affects customers is important!

109.

*Avoid disappointment or misunderstandings:
make it easy for people to give you what you
want or need from them.*

110.

*Sales is service—service is sales.
Great sales and service result in
customers who are sold on you.*

111.

If customer service were a competitive event, where would you be in the rankings?

112.

When you have frustrating experiences, don't keep track. Instead, only count your positive experiences.

113.

*People hate to wait: a prompt partial
solution is often better than a full
resolution that takes a long time.*

114.

*What if moods were contagious?
What would people catch from you?*

115.

A smile you have to "put" on your face is still superior to an earnest, sincere, heartfelt frown.

116.

Customers may not always be right, but pointing it out to them can be a wrong move.

117.

Even if you can't immediately wait on a
customer, connect with your eyes, smile,
and nod. Let them know you've noticed them.

118.

The behaviors you practice at work end
up becoming habits. What habits are
you working on every day?

119.

In working with people, listen to your heart. In working with problems, listen to your head.

120.

Attitude is what makes a boring job fun or a fun job boring.

121.

When you're on the phone, smile. Your voice always sounds exactly like your face looks.

122.

In service, as in life, what goes around comes around. Only give out to your customers and coworkers what you want given back to you!

123.

You're in charge of where your mind goes. You don't let your feet take you to places you don't want to go—why let your mind do it?

124.

When the game of service is played right, everyone comes out a winner.

125.

When problems surface, negative people give up. Positive people give it one more try.

126.

How others treat you reflects their character. How you treat others reflects your character.

127.

When it comes to service experiences, keep the positives in front of you and the negatives behind.

128.

You can't force people to be nice but your behavior can be a positive force in encouraging them to be nice.

129.

When something bad happens that you can't change, remember that you can accept a situation without having to approve of it.

130.

Ignore the people who try to make you feel bad about feeling good. Since when do you have to apologize for having a good day?

131.

Those who think the world is boring
are boring to be around.

132.

Communication is important, and the
most important conversations of all
are the ones that go on in your mind.

133.

Rather than watching the clock, keep your eye on what needs to be done.

134.

Your mind and body are connected: every now and then, give yourself a mental and physical boost. Smile!

135.

*In the absence of feedback, customers
make up their own version of reality.
Keep them informed and updated.*

136.

*You can't always know why people
behave as they do, but you can know
why you do!*

137.

In customer service you have only two major concerns—what goes on in your head and what comes out of your mouth!

138.

It pays to enjoy what you do for a living. If you enjoy your work, just think— you're being paid to have fun!

139.

Service is both an art and a science. The art is in knowing what to do with customers, and the science is in knowing when to do it.

140.

When you make an effort to help other people, you benefit more than they do.

141.

An extra minute with a customer right now can save you hours down the road.

142.

Whether you work for a company or non-profit organization, you have customers. And customers are why your job exists.

notes

Service Skills
in
Action

The Charles Law of Opposites

You may occasionally experience a perfect workday but, more likely, your daily events range from positive to negative, comic to conflicting, fun to frustrating. You're no stranger to what I've named the Law of Opposites.

Here's an explanation: for every positive intent or well prepared strategy, there exists an equal amount of resistance or inertia that interferes with the ideal. In other words, whatever you plan or strive for, the exact opposite outcome often happens. Maybe you can identify with the following examples:

On the days you plan to get lots of extra work done you will experience the most interruptions.

The fewer people on staff at any given time, the heavier the customer traffic will be.

When stress goes up, cooperation goes down.

The less time you have to wait on a customer, the more questions that customer will have.

The customers who most need your patience will be the most irritating or difficult to deal with.

The more you need support or assistance, the more reluctant you will be to ask for it.

On the days you most need to be patient, your mental fuse will be its shortest.

The customers who are the most emotionally needy will be the least likable and the most demanding.

Understanding the **Law of Opposites** gives you an edge in tough service situations. Your optimistic attitude, sense of humor, positive persistence, and flexibility will help you prevail every time, whether at work or home.

Self-Talk:
Handling the Stress of Service

One of the factors in lowering your work stress is accepting the fact that you live in a less than perfect world and many things lie outside of your command. And while you can't control everything that happens, you *can* control how you react.

We've established that maintaining a positive outlook helps you perceive problems as challenges and obstacles as opportunities. The following statements will help you keep your perspective the next time you face a less than ideal situation.

I recognize that providing service for my customers creates a certain amount of inconvenience, stress, or interpersonal conflict. I need to accept that this is the nature of work and doing business.

I acknowledge that we all make mistakes despite our best intentions, and it is self-defeating and stressful to hold this against my customers, coworkers, manager, or myself.

I know that at work (and at home) things won't always happen the way I want, and I accept that wishing things were different won't make them so.

I recognize that it is often people's negative behaviors (anger, blame, denial, accusation, retaliation) that surface during stressful times and that I cannot change or control people's defensive reactions.

I possess the knowledge, skill, and mental hardiness to initiate positive behavior changes, and I am capable of overcoming my initial resistance when attempting personal change.

I am capable of learning from every challenging situation in which I find myself, and the quality of what I learn and how I apply it is up to me.

I know that while I can't control what happens to me, how I react to stressful events or people's demands is entirely my call. I alone choose my thoughts, feelings, and actions.

In spite of life's imperfections, frustrations, or conflicts, I can choose to strive, thrive, and celebrate being alive. I set my own mood every day.

Seven Benefits of a Smile

1. Smiling lowers your blood pressure.
2. It gives your metabolism a boost.
3. Smiling produces endorphins (happy hormones).
4. It decreases your stress level and helps you relax.
5. When you smile, your oxygen level increases.
6. Smiling assists your digestion.
7. And it helps keep your immune system tuned up.

Some people think that you should "smile for others" but your smile is actually for YOU!

146.

Physical Energizers: Reducing Your Work Stress

Throughout your work day—**STOP**—every now and then and take a nice deep breath. Do a quick "body check;" find the tight, tense areas and release your tension. Consciously relax.

Whenever you find yourself feeling rushed and stressed, force yourself to—**STOP**—so you can slow down. Consciously release your tension: relax your forehead, jaw, shoulders, and hands.

SMILE—to yourself and briefly think of something positive and pleasant.

Take a moment—**FOCUS**—and concentrate on your breathing. Take a nice, deep, long breath from your diaphragm rather than your chest, inhaling very slowly and exhaling very slowly. Envision clean air and energy entering your body on the inhale, and stress exiting your body on the exhale.

After two deep breaths—**RELAX**—and be quiet for just a moment. Pace yourself through the day with these periodic energizers and you'll find your stress and tension replaced with energy and enthusiasm.

147.

Mental Energizers:
Enhancing Your Attitude

Keep smiling: it feels great to you, looks great to others, and even sounds great on the phone!

Train yourself to think positive, constructive thoughts while consciously banishing negative ones.

Just as water naturally rolls off a duck's back, let people's bad moods just naturally roll off your back.

Lighten up! Worry less, laugh more, slow down.

Every day, look for what's right rather than what's wrong. Focus on what's worth appreciating rather than agonizing over what you cannot control.

Sincerely compliment others when they do a good job (including your manager).

Remind yourself that opportunity accompanies every adversity: meet your challenges head on.

Communicate to people's strengths rather than their weaknesses to foster teamwork and cooperation.

Think like a winner. World Class athletes summon their best skills when the chips are down and they deliver. You can too!

Understanding the Nature of Human Nature

• Most people want to be helpful and cooperative most of the time.

• It's our insecurities, not our strengths, that tend to surface when we're under pressure.

• When things break down between people, it's usually a matter of differing perceptions.

• When people feel desperate they often do things to get their way that they would not otherwise do.

• People often get self-protective and defensive when conflicts arise—they may accuse or blame rather than listen or admit to their mistake.

• The more wrong someone is, the more "right" she or he may try to be.

• The more we care about a situation, the more difficult it is for us to remain objective.

149.

Beware: "No Zone" Alert

While cities may announce ozone alerts, we'd like to present our **No Zone** alert! If you've read the first section of this book, you already know that we can instantly alienate customers and turn them into adversaries by using words such as:

I can't help you...
You didn't follow the proper procedure...
We can't do that...
We can't make any exceptions...
We're not allowed to...
It's against policy...
That's not my job...

Stay clear of the **No Zone** by emphasizing what you *can do* for you customers. The fewer *no's* you use, the more your customers will say *yes* to you!

When You Must Say No

We've introduced the idea of avoiding the **No Zone**, so when you must say "no" you want to do it in the most positive manner possible.

Remember, when customers hear the words, "I can't..." they often think it means "I won't!" Explain briefly and non-defensively why such a policy exists and how it benefits the customer. By the way, if there's no benefit for the customer, why do you do it?

"We established this policy for customer confidentiality. You can be assured we'd do the same for you." Or try *"We needed to modify this policy after we discovered..."*

When possible, offer an alternative solution to help customers feel better about not getting exactly what they want.

While you want to sound apologetic, avoid being excessive about it. Too many excuses make you sound defensive, and too much apology makes you appear wrong. Even the words "I'm sorry" can make it sound as if you are personally responsible. A simple "I apologize" is more accurate. Otherwise the customer may begin thinking that you should actually be doing more than you are.

Express disappointment when you are unable to meet the customer's request. *"I wish there were more I could do..."* Show empathy by saying, *"I appreciate your understanding..."* Be prepared to repeat yourself if necessary, because it's hard for people to listen when they're experiencing stress or frustration.

Express a sincere desire to help the person even if there is little or nothing else you can do right now. Express positive expectations for the future. *"Perhaps in the future we will have more options..."* And once again, thank the customer for understanding.

When the Customer is Wrong

Earlier in *The Companion,* we discussed the idea that while customers are often wrong, there is no future in making them feel wrong. You will get further with people if you are tactful, diplomatic, and able to deflect their objections or arguments.

The following approaches are equally effective in both spoken and written communication.

Respond with a neutral statement first:
I appreciate your asking about that...
Other people have been under that impression...
I know other customers who thought that, too…

And then gently correct the customer's perceptions:
Actually, what you really need to do is...
The correct procedure is...
Here's the situation in a nutshell…

Let the customer know the next step in the process.
So once we get this information from you we should be able to…
Now that you understand exactly what we need, we can go ahead and…
So all we need to do now is…

Express your appreciation and anticipation of a positive outcome.
I do appreciate your flexibility…
I think you'll be pleased with the results…
Perhaps in the future we will have more options…

In customer service, it pays to keep things simple and cordial. These examples will help you do that, every step of the way. Remember—the better you handle a situation, the more likely your customer will too!

152.

Dealing With Feelings

Whether you are communicating on the phone or in person, when someone is upset or angry you want to resolve matters quickly, efficiently, and objectively. Here are a few things to keep in mind:

• If you're on the phone, use gestures as you speak; it helps you channel your nervous energy.

• Direct the conversation through relevant questions or restatement:
Could you repeat that number...
In other words, you're asking...
So what you need from us is...

• Accept the upset person's emotional state as a display of concern. Work at staying neutral and objective rather than becoming irritated or critical.

• Sincerely want to help; remind yourself that any attempt to make the customer wrong is self-defeating. If you win the battle, you lose the war.

• "Stop" questions are a way of giving the customer a quick task to do. This can interrupt their anger and divert their energy toward problem solving. *I want to verify your account number to make sure I recorded it correctly; would you repeat it…*
Again, the date of service was_____; is that correct?

• If you're on the phone and you begin feeling intimidated, take a deep breath, sit up straight, use larger gestures, and if all else fails, stand up!

Words That Reflect a Service Attitude

Please...

Thank you...

How may I help you...

I'm happy to help...

Tell me more...

Yes, that is unfortunate...

I think I can understand how that affected you...

I regret that you were inconvenienced...

I can appreciate that...

I am unable to do that, but here's what I can do...

Thank you for taking the time to let me know...

I do apologize...

Let's see what we can do...

We had no idea a customer might get that impression...

I don't know the answer right now, but I'd be happy to find out for you...

154.

These Are Not Questions

In serving or selling customers you need to ask exploratory, involving questions. Elsewhere in *The Companion*, we've explained that "what" and "how" questions are very effective. However, the commonly used phrases below are neither questions nor are they effective!

Isn't it... Doesn't it... Don't you think...
Aren't you... Shouldn't you...

Although they may sound like questions, they are actually statements of opinion. Note that each one contains a "not." People often use these phrases to subtly blame, insinuate, or control. Pay close attention to how it feels when someone uses one with you and you'll quickly figure out how they could backfire with a customer!

155.

Dealing With Upset People Without Getting Upset

Working with upset or unhappy customers is part of your job, and as with everything else, your attitude is essential. It also bears repeating that these strategies for handling conflict and misunderstandings will help you both at work and home.

Think of an upset customer as someone who really needs your help. Here is a mini-manual on how to "keep it together" during a tense interaction.

Step One. Relax; breathe. We tend to hold our breath when we get tense. Sit or stand straight and relax. If you look relaxed you will feel more relaxed. Lengthen your spine rather than "scrunch up." Release your shoulders; keep your hands open and relaxed. Breathe. Look the person in the eye. Keep your facial muscles neutral: avoid frowning.

Step Two. Listen to both words and feelings so you can fully understand the customer's position. Let people ventilate and explain what they're upset about. When it's your turn to respond, gather your thoughts before you speak. Avoid sounding defensive. To the customer, what should have been, could have been, or would have been is irrelevant.

People get irritated with lengthy explanations. Repeat key words or phrases to indicate you have heard and understood the other party's remarks. Offer solutions or options rather than excuses or explanations, and communicate your willingness to explore and resolve the situation.

Step Three. Stay objective: don't take things personally. Consider the customer's position. Remember that we all perceive the world differently, and most conflict represents a difference in perception rather than right versus wrong. Accept the other party's interpretation as simply *different* from yours.

Step Four. Take whatever steps you can to resolve the situation and explain your plan to the customer. Avoid silent arguments, judgments, and mental "duelogue." Maintain a neutral to friendly attitude and remind yourself this is an important part of your job. Focus on how good it feels to manage a difficult situation skillfully.

Step Five. Keep your ego low so you can better empathize with others. When ego gets involved, empathy disappears. You can tell the minute your ego gets hooked because you'll get hung up on "being right" instead of "going for results."

Step Six. Anticipate that you will occasionally face upset people and that these experiences will help keep your communication skills sharp. Stay "in shape" for service. Eat a moderate, healthy diet, exercise regularly, get proper amounts of sleep. Life is short. Work hours are "life" hours. Make them all count!

156.

One Dozen Ways to Communicate Quality Service

1. Maintain a consistently positive attitude and show it with your smile and friendly manner.

2. Offer a positive, professional appearance (dress, posture, facial expression, neat work area).

3. Respond to customers promptly or at least immediately acknowledge their presence if you are momentarily occupied.

4. Use courteous words: *please, thank you, that's a good choice, I appreciate that…*

5. If the phone rings when you're with a customer, excuse yourself first and answer it by the second ring. Keep the call brief and cordial, and maintain eye contact with the customer who is in front of you.

6. To "connect" with customers, ask appropriate questions about their needs and listen carefully to the answers, especially if you are selling.

7. To get good treatment from others, give it. Treat your coworkers, supervisor, or manager just as you do your customers.

8. When customers are upset, show empathy and honest concern for their situation.

9. Remember people's names. Keep records and notes of special information about customers if you will be serving them again.

10. If you promise to follow up, do so. Simple courtesy and thoughtfulness are very impressive.

11. When customers ask for directions, guide them to the area rather than simply pointing.

12. If you're feeling rushed, keep practicing your service skills, even if you have a long line of people waiting. If you are competent, calm, and friendly they'll pick up on your mood and feel more confident in your ability to handle the situation.

Remember, unless you have magical powers, you can only wait on one person at a time. So if you help each customer feel singled out and important, those in line will know that's the kind of service they'll receive when you wait on them. Standing in line may be an irritation to customers but the expectation of your warm friendly service gives them something to look forward to.

13. Give each of your customers just a little bit more than they expected (just as I have done with this list). Keep trying to outdo yourself (athletes call it going for their Personal Best), and you'll continually raise your standards of performance. You will become a customer service champion!

When You're on the Phone, You're on the Line

Telephone skills are essential to good service, but many people take them for granted. Consider:

- For some customers, the telephone is their only contact with your organization. Always answer the phone as soon as possible, preferably by the second ring. Enunciate and speak directly into the mouthpiece. Keep a pad of paper and pen handy so you can take messages or make notes.

- For calls from both the outside and inside, try a cordial, "Thank you for calling _____, this is _____, how may I help you?" If you work the switchboard, it is unnecessary to identify yourself.

- Smile! It relaxes your vocal chords. Try to

sound fresh and friendly, regardless of how long you have been on your shift. You may be answering your "umpty umpth" call, but it's the caller's first!

• Keep your voice tone animated. Refrain from trying to read, file, or work on your computer while on the phone. Splitting your attention this way compromises your vocal quality, and you'll end up sounding tired or uninterested.

• Listen carefully and concentrate on the call. Avoid rushing or interrupting the caller unless you need to ask for a name, account number, date, or other necessary information.

• If you take a message, repeat it back to the caller to make sure it's correct. If you make any promises or need to take any kind of action, do it! Your reputation, and that of your organization, is on the line.

• Avoid telephone tag. If you need to leave a message, give a best time of day to reach you. If you will be away for an extended period, it's common courtesy to let the party know.

When leaving messages, clearly and briefly explain the nature of your call so people can respond even if you will be out when they call back. Consider requesting a fax number and sending a written message so the person you're trying to reach can conveniently reply.

• Some people slam the receiver down or switch to another line the minute their call is finished, and that's a mistake. Always let the other party hang up first, or make it appear that way by hanging up in a two-step process.

Step one: Hold the phone a few inches from your ear and hesitate a second or two. *Step two:* Gently hang up the phone. This unique technique adds a truly professional tone to your call!

158.

More Telephone Tips

Telephone communication is challenging because you lack all of the visual cues so helpful in face-to-face communication. To offset this important missing information you need to develop some special skills and techniques. Here are some more tips for using the telephone effectively.

• People first, paper second works on the phone as well as in person; take a moment to build instant rapport before you get down to business.

• Envision what the person might look like; this helps you sound more natural. Gesture if that is normal for you; the energy you generate will be reflected in your voice.

• Before transferring, tell callers who they will

be speaking with, and give them the number or extension before attempting the transfer. This way, if they are accidently cut off, they can call back direct.

• When a caller needs to speak with someone other than you, simply transfer the call or get the proper party. If you ever, for any reason, need to interrupt a caller, do so by saying, "I need to interrupt you..." It's okay to interrupt if you first tell the person you're going to!

• If an upset caller needs to speak with a coworker, "warn" whomever will take the call *before* they get on the line with the customer. It's a good idea to explain the customer's situation to your coworker so the customer doesn't have to repeat their tale of woe, and become upset, yet again!

• When putting callers on hold, if it will be a long wait, clarify that. Give people an option to hang up if that will be more convenient for them, once you agree who will call back, and when. If you put a caller on extended hold, be sure to check back every 30 seconds or so.

• If someone calls you by mistake, you can save them embarrassment or irritation by saying, *"You need to speak with…"* rather than *"You have the wrong department."* You can easily grasp how the first statement helps the caller feel better, and such diplomacy makes you look better, too!

• Wait one extra ring to gather yourself if you have just had a tense or upsetting interaction. First, take a deep "cleansing" breath, and let all the tension go. Now you are ready to smile, answer the phone, and start anew.

How to *L.I.S.T.E.N.* to Upset Customers

Let the person explain.
Simply listen. When people are upset they need to ventilate before they are ready to hear anything you have to say. And you need to fully understand their situation before you can help. You will always accomplish more by listening from the customer's point of view.

Investigate the situation thoroughly.
Get all the facts so you can know exactly what has happened and what needs to be done next. Unless the person is completely unreasonable, only interrupt to ask for relevant information. Avoid defending yourself, your coworkers, or your organization. Remain neutral, open, helpful, and interested in the customer's situation.

State that you want to help.
In the midst of a problem or conflict, people often feel misunderstood. A positive statement from you such as, *"Helping you is a part of my job..."* or simply, *"I'd like to help you take care of this..."* suggests to customers that their situation is valid and worth listening to.

Talk in a calm, sincere manner.
Keep your tone controlled without being falsely calm and let your warmth or concern come through. Focus on the customer's concerns as you speak. Your attitude is essential. Avoid blame or insinuation.

Empathize with the customer.
View the situation from the customer's perspective. Listen for feelings and perceptions, not just words. When dealing with upset people, try to identify with their reality as best you can while you work to resolve the dispute.

Neutralize the atmosphere by remaining positive. View a conflict not as a problem, but as an opportunity to help someone in need. People don't consciously mean to be difficult and demanding, but sometimes situations get the best of them. Your positive attitude will help make the **L.I.S.T.E.N.** process work—for your customers, and for you!

Good P.R. Means Personal Responsibility

Whether your job is primarily service or sales, there are times when you'll do everything right with customers but they may still be angry or upset. You know you cannot control other people's perceptions and behavior, you can only control your own. In these instances, it helps to focus on what you did *right* rather than obsessing over a customer's bad attitude.

Service is largely a public relations campaign, and when you behave responsibly, chances are, you've done your best. Here's to Service PR—Personal Rights accompanied by Personal Responsibilities.

While we all want to be treated with respect we are also responsible for showing respect to other people, even when they aren't showing the same level of respect for us at the moment.

We all make mistakes. Our customers will make mistakes and so will we. No one is perfect. Each of us is responsible for doing a good job, and at the same time, we need to accept the consequences of our behavior when we err. This way, we can each learn from our mistakes.

We all want to be listened to and taken seriously by others, and this means we are responsible for listening to, and taking our customer's concerns seriously, regardless of who they are.

We all want the freedom to ask questions, to make requests, and express our opinions or dissatisfaction. We are also responsible for the judgments we make about others when they express themselves in a less than perfect manner.

We each have our own unique perspective and we are responsible for how we express our perceptions and reactions. At the same time, we are responsible for how we regard the perceptions of others.

We all want things to run smoothly and conveniently, and we are responsible for how we behave when things don't go as we would like. Each of us can be a winner or a whiner. It's a choice!

161.

A Quick Service Assessment

Here are two good question to ask—and answer—in a staff meeting; but only ask them if you plan on taking action:

How are we perceived by our customers?

How do we want to be perceived by them?

If there is a difference between the two, you have your work cut out for you!

Service Assignments

Here are some challenging projects for you and your service team:

• In a staff meeting, working as a group, identify the occasions when you must say "no" to your customers. Then as a group, devise a few ways to say "no" positively—without using the words, *no, not, don't, can't*—and pledge to use them.

• Hold a customer service "Inside Out" contest. Investigate your workplace and see who can come up with the longest list of circumstances that confuse, mislead, irritate, or inconvenience your customers. And then find ways to eliminate the problems.

• Make excellent service a part of your culture by joining the International Customer Service Association and celebrating Customer Service Week.

- Emphasize teamwork and internal service just as you do external service because, as you know, customer service starts on the inside.

- In staff meetings or on your own, *practice* your customer service skills so they'll come out of your mouth automatically when you face an upset customer.

- Encourage everyone in your department to do what they can to help create a positive, productive work environment where service is fun, fulfilling, and rewarding.

- Identify your internal service "champions." Invite them to teach what they know and encourage everyone to learn from those who practice excellent service skills every day.

Have You H.U.G.G.E.D. a Customer Today?

Have you…

Helped your customer beyond normal expectations?

Understood exactly the nature of his or her needs?

Gathered critical information by thoroughly exploring the customer's situation?

Given the customer a chance to talk while you listen?

Empathized with the customer's position if there was a problem or unique circumstance?

Developed a trusting relationship so your customer will be motivated to return?

Every customer deserves to be **H.U.G.G.E.D.**

164.

The 4R Method
for Fast Recovery

It can be stressful listening to complaints, criticism, or conflicting perceptions, yet it is part of your job. Here's one way you can quickly recover from service stress and refocus on the positive parts of your job.

Relax. Once the stressful interaction is over, take a nice deep cleansing breath and let your body **relax.** Now that the situation is over, it's in your best interest to let it go. Remind yourself that you can "hear it and clear it." Release any tightness or tension in your face and shoulders and take another nice, deep breath.

Review. Take a moment to **review** what just happened. Immediately make notes or take whatever prompt follow-up action you promised. Considering what you now know, determine how you might handle a similar situation in the future. Identify one thing you'd do differently, and one thing you feel good about having done.

Resolve. Remind yourself that while you cannot control how other people feel or behave, you are totally and completely in charge of how you feel and behave. **Resolve** to remain objective and forget your bad feelings so you can effectively move on to more important issues.

Reset. Now that the situation is over, **reset** your attitude. You know that replaying a past situation is self-defeating, stressful, and an unproductive use of your time. Consciously choose to let it go and move forward. You can reset your attitude as often as you need to. Smile and give yourself a compliment. You deserve it!

4R means Recovery:
Relax, Review, Resolve, Reset.

Customer Service: as Simple as A - B - C

A is for promptly **Acknowledging** every customer's presence.

B is for **Being** there for each of your customers.

C is for making the **Commitment** to meet customer needs on a timely basis.

D is for **Deflecting** negative customer comments or complaints so you can resolve the issue.

E is for **Elevating** your service and overall work performance to new levels.

F is for a **Friendly** face: yours!

G is for **Going** the extra mile.

H is for making yourself (and others) **Happy** while you work.

I is for **Individuality**. Your individual efforts influence customer perceptions.

J is for **Just** doing your job, in a consistently positive, professional manner.

K is for the **Kindness** you show each customer, whether internal or external.

L is for **Lightening** up so you can keep the pressure low and the pleasure high.

M is for **Making** the choice to do your best in each and every customer transaction.

N is for the **New** attitude you bring to work each and every day.

O is for **Opening** your mind to new, improved ways of doing your job.

P is for **Present**: your ability to stay "in the moment" helps prevent blame, worry, or anxiety.

Q is for the **Quality** you bring to your workplace and your personal life, too.

R is for the **Relaxation** breaks you give yourself, especially after tense moments.

S is for sustaining your **Spirit** with positive thoughts and a pleasant smile.

T is for taking extra **Time** with customers who need special attention or assistance.

U is for **Understanding** that while people can sometimes ruin a moment, only you can ruin your day.

V is for **Value**. You add value to every transaction when you do your best.

W is for the inner **Wisdom** you practice when you do right by others.

X is for the **eXtra** effort you expend to creatively solve a problem.

Y is for **You**, because *you* make the choice to practice your service skills.

Z is for **Zest**. The more you practice the Customer Service Alphabet, the more zest you will have for your work, and your personal life, too.

About the Author

There are consultants, speakers, and business professionals who position and label themselves as "topic experts" and then there are those who simply, quietly, consistently, and successfully go about their business. No fanfare, no fancy marketing ploys, no overt gimmicks or high pressure tactics; they simply live the example. Leslie Charles is one of those people.

Since the mid-seventies, Leslie Charles has made her living as a speaker and consultant, first as a community college instructor, and then as president of her company, TRAININGWORKS. While she has never actively marketed her speaking and consulting services, Leslie's distinguished career spans the North American continent and twenty years.

With an impressive list of repeat clients from both private and public sector, from small nonprofit agencies to large corporations and associations, Leslie personifies the power of "word of mouth" advertising. Her satisfied customers not only hire her back—they happily tell others about her!

What's her secret? Service, plain and simple. With an eye for detail and an unflagging enthusiasm for doing what's right, Leslie practices all of the ideas and principles in The *Customer Service Companion,* and more! She possesses an uncanny ability to connect with her audience members—her customers—in a unique and unforgettable way.

If there's room for improvement in your service staff or delivery systems, come to the source. Leslie Charles is available for keynotes, seminars, and consultations. Bring her to your organization where she will personally work with your employees and guarantee an effective, memorable, customized presentation that's geared just for you!

To invite Leslie to your organization or to inquire about programs call: 1-800-670-7535
E-mail LesChas@aol.com

Product Information

If your budget prevents you from bringing Leslie Charles to your organization, your best option is an autographed set of *The Customer Service Companion* and *The Companion Study Guide* for each member of your sales or service team. These tools will enable you to conduct your own ongoing service seminar. Our quantity pricing makes it possible for every employee to have their own personal set of *The Companions*.

You might also enjoy Leslie's highly praised *STICK TO IT! The Power of Positive Persistence*—an inspirational resource for busy people who like to stay positive and motivated.

Also available: our quality embossed, red and gold Lapel Pin, the perfect fashion accessory for the positive person; silver and red foil *STICK TO IT!* stickers and Leslie's Minspirations, 12 inspirational miniposters: original poems and writings printed on colorful designer papers, suitable for framing.

To order products, simply photocopy the order form and send it along with your payment. Or call us toll free at 1-800-670-7535.

Yes! Press
PO Box 956, East Lansing, MI 48826
1-800-670-7535

The Customer Service Companion @ $10.95   ____copies

The Companion Study Guide @ $6.95   ____copies

*STICK TO IT! by C. Leslie Charles @ $11.95*____copies

STICK TO IT! Elegant Lapel Pin @ $5.95   ____pins

STICK TO IT! 36 Deluxe Foil Seals @ $5.95   ____packs

Minspirations—12 miniposters @ $11.95   ____sets

Shipping is $3.50 for single items.
**Order three or more items—in any combination,
sent to one address—and we'll pay the postage!**

I've enclosed payment of _____

Name: _____

Address:_____

_____

_____

Phone: _____